Genesis Of Love

By Shane W. Schofield

ISBN: 979-8-9892068-0-3 (Digital)

ISBN: 979-8-9892068-1-0 (Paperback)

ISBN: 979-8-9892068-2-7 (Hardcover)

This book of poems draws fictional inspiration from biblical stories, offering artistic interpretations and symbolism. It does not provide definitive religious teachings or challenge any beliefs. Readers are encouraged to approach it as a work of fiction, respecting diverse interpretations and finding appreciation for the power of storytelling and poetry.

Front cover image by Dale Snell.

Book design by Shane Schofield.

First digital edition 2023.

Published by Shane Wesley Schofield

81634 420th St

Truman, MN 56088

Twitter: *@RealGenOfLove*

ABOUT THE AUTHOR

Shane Wesley Schofield is a poet and novelist, weaving words with the finesse of a seasoned wordsmith. With a unique perspective shaped by being one of four living half-Shelties, half-South Dakotans, his writing transports readers to worlds where imagination intertwines with the extraordinary.

Growing up in the vast landscapes of South Dakota, Shane developed a deep appreciation for nature and the power of storytelling at a young age. Drawing inspiration from his dual heritage, he skillfully blends the ethereal qualities of the Sheltie spirit with the rugged sensibilities of the Dakotan heartland, creating narratives that resonate on both personal and universal levels.

As a poet, Shane's verses dance on the page, capturing moments of love, loss, and the complexities of the human experience. Each line is infused with an emotional intensity that lingers, touching the depths of the soul.

When Shane isn't crafting captivating stories, he can be found producing renewable energy in Minnesota, or singing classic songs with new and improved lyrics at the lake with his children.

Connect with Shane Wesley Schofield and explore his literary realm by following him on social media. Prepare to be transported to worlds where words soar, emotions ignite, and the ordinary becomes extraordinary.

Twitter: *@RealGenOfLove*

DEDICATION

This book is dedicated to my parents, my siblings, and my children.

Dad, I've spent the first 40 years of my life emulating your example because you are the greatest man I have ever met.

Mom, your kindness touches everyone around you. I would not be the person I am today if not for you.

Donna, you are the very best sister that a brother could ever have.

Eddie, I finally found the song about the lizards!

Sergeant Charles A. Schofield, please forgive me for the Tabasco pancakes. I had no idea you would grow up to be top of your class in the U.S. Marines, or I swear I wouldn't have done it!

Jack, you've worked so hard on your education. I'm proud of you, son!

Ryan, I hope that this book shows you that when something bad happens in life, it can help to write a poem making fun of Satan, the first being in all the history of the universe to be a LOSER!

Katie, when the world started descending into darkness, God blessed me with a daughter who has brightened every one of my days!

I love you all!

ACKNOWLEDGEMENTS

Firstly, I want to thank The Lord for creating the heavens and the earth. I also want to thank Him for creating my Greatest Grandpa Adam and Greatest Grandma Eve. I cannot overstate how happy I am that I have the opportunity to experience life!

Due to the nature of this particular book, I find myself needing to acknowledge some people who have passed away quite a while ago. I must thank Moses for actually writing Genesis. As hard as the world works to corrupt the past, I sincerely doubt an oral tradition would have survived intact to reach my ears. I also want to thank Noah for building that ark! When you stop to think about it, each and every one of us were riding along with him.

I also want to thank my illustrator, Dale Snell, and my editor, Silvestra Z. Griffin who have been tremendously helpful as I work towards publishing this book. Without them, this book would probably never have been released. Thank you!

BEFORE

Before

It was forever

Or maybe never

There was no time

But the Father

And His Spirit

And His Word

Did all opine

Eternal moment

Without direction

Only perfection

Limits creativity

So in Their union,

Did They decide

To open wide

Creation, to set love free

In the beginning, all was dark

A void, a stillness, not a spark

But the Creator felt a stirring

A desire for something more than blurring

He pondered, mused, and wondered too,

What if He spoke something new?

A world of light, of life, of sound,

with creatures great and small around.

He shaped the stars,

He formed the planets,

He breathed into existence

all the rabbits,

The birds, the bees,

The fish, the bears,

And from the dust,

Humans to care.

He crafted every

Flower and tree,

With every stroke,

His joy did spree,

A masterpiece of boundless wonder,

A world to ponder,

Time not to squander.

And so it was,

the universe came to be,

a canvas for all to see,

God's love and power,

His grace and might,

forever shining

in the day and night.

HOSTS

In the presence of the Lord,

I stand.

My wings in awe,

my heart in His hand

A light so bright

A love so pure

A beauty that's complete

And sure.

The joy of heaven

fills my soul

as I bask in the glory

of the Almighty's role

I am but a servant

A humble one

A witness to the wonders

that He has done

The choir of angels

sings His praise

Our voices a symphony

that never fades

And all around,

we heavenly hosts,

rejoice in our eternal

heavenly posts

In His embrace,

I feel complete

A joy that makes

my heart skip a beat

And as I gaze

upon His face

I see a love

that never fades.

But as I stand

in this divine embrace,

a shadow falls;

a chilling space.

Lucifer

Once bright, now dark

Comes with lies,

to make his mark.

I hear his whispers

his deceitful words

that turn my heart

like angry birds

But I remain

steadfast in faith.

And hold on

to the Lord's embrace.

For I know,

His love is true.

And with His strength,

I can renew

My commitment

to His holy name;

And rise above

the tempter's game.

So I stand firm

in His love and grace,

knowing that

in this holy place

I am safe

I am secure

In the presence of my Lord

Forevermore.

FELL

Once the favored Archangel, I was

In God's grace, I never had a pause

A bright and shining star in the sky

With a heart full of love, no lie.

I followed His will without question,

A humble servant, without objection,

My heart filled with love and gratitude,

For the blessings that He bestowed with magnitude.

From my honored position

above the Lord's throne,

taking His bright glory

refracting colors that shone

In a brilliance bedazzling all who beheld

As the Saphiric Ocean in colors did swell

I mean, of course, His Face radiates brilliant light

But isn't it boring when all of it is white?

Why wouldn't pride within me grow?

A desire for more, a hunger to show

That I was more than just a mere Archangel

That my talents and skills were more than a spangle.

I realized after all that I'm superior

And my devotion to God became inferior

I thought I could start doing things my way

And that my ideas were better than His every day

But still, I kept it hidden from view

Afraid of what God and the others would do

I played along, I kept the façade

Until it became too much, I could no longer dodge.

What is truth?

After all, what had He done?

He created in me

His own superior son!

The pride within me began to take hold

And my loyalty to God began to fold

I started to whisper my doubts to my peers

And soon, I found myself playing on their hopes and their fears

I became consumed by my own pride

And in my heart,

His love slowly died

Seems I had grown just too smart

I knew I could be the ruler of all

And that my power would never ever fall

I rebelled against God

I betrayed Him,

I gathered angels to fight

I knew clearly I'd win

Disbelief

As I learned

I was actually wrong

I learned that my pride

had lied

To me all along!

I was cast out

Banished from heaven's sight

My once bright light

now veiled in night

My heart consumed

by anger and hate

How DARE God punish me

For choices He created me to make!

I fell to the depths

of hell's abyss

A place of darkness

of pain, and of hiss

And there, I raged, and I seethed

Against the God who I once believed.

But even in my wrath

and my despair

I won't concede that pride was my snare

I had lost everything I held dear

But I'll have my revenge

Then I'll smile and sneer.

I realize the error of my way

There never was any hope for me to sway

God's love was not something I could overcome and win

For pride was the root of all my sin.

Now to regroup, plan a new strategy

Then all of us Demons will victoriously

Throw off God's chains, and then we will be free

I've wept for the love that I had lost

For the price that my pride had cost

For my station that I can never restore

For the Heavens that I would never explore.

As I lay in my fiery pit

I fear that my fate was sealed and writ

My pride started me down this road

I risk eternally suffering in my eternal abode

But I see in Eden that God has made men,

If I'm to suffer down here, I will do so with them!

So still, I raged against the night

Against the love that I had lost in sight

Against the God who had cast me out

For the pride that had made me shout.

I screamed in anger, I cursed His name

I blamed Him for my eternal flame

For the pain and the suffering I had to bear

For the love that I could no longer share

Deep down, sure I know that some blame is for me

I acted too soon, causing my own misery

I loved all the praise I would daily receive

Which soon clouded my views, and what I should believe

Love isn't something that should ever be earned

My privilege will be a whole Universe I govern

My cunning, my strategy, it will blind God's sight

I'll be the new god of the Universe; this is my birthright!

CREATE

In the beginning, there was nothing but void,

A darkness that enveloped all, unalloyed,

But then I spoke, and there was light,

And the darkness gave way to the dawn, so bright.

I created the heavens, the earth, and the seas,

The mountains, the rivers, the birds, and the bees,

And I saw that it was good, just as I had planned,

A perfect home for all, a fresh wonderland.

I breathed life into the soil, and it stirred,

And out of the dust, I created man and bird,

Each with a purpose, a destiny, a plan,

A reflection of my love, my wisdom, my hand.

I watched as the world unfolded before my eyes,

As the creatures roamed, and the plants did rise,

And I saw that it was good, just as I had said,

A place of beauty, of wonder, of life's thread.

But man, in his free will, made a choice,

And with it, came a pain, a sorrow, a voice,

And the world, once perfect, became flawed,

As sin, death, and the devil tried to become god.

But still, I loved the world that I had made,

So I called on my son, to heal and to save,

To offer hope, to redeem, to restore,

The beauty of the world, that was lost before.

And so, the earth will soon be redeemed,

By the love of the One who created, who beamed,

The light that shone, in the darkness of old,

And the story of creation, forever told.

IMAGE

In my image,

I created man,

From dust and breath,

my perfect plan,

A being of wonder,

of beauty, of light,

A reflection of my love,

my power, my might.

I formed his body

with my hands,

With care and love,

I made him lands,

And in his eyes,

I saw a spark,

A glimpse of the life,

that would soon embark.

I gave him a heart

that beats with mine,

A soul that reflects

My divine,

And in his mind,

I placed a seed,

Of knowledge, of wisdom,

of all he would need.

I breathed into his nostrils,

the breath of life,

And he opened his eyes,

to a world without strife,

And as he stood,

 a new creation,

I saw my purpose,

my joy, my elation.

I gave him a name,

Adam, he was,

A being of wonder,

of grace, of cause,

And in the garden,

he walked with me.

In perfect communion,

in perfect harmony.

And so, in Adam,

I saw my plan,

To share my love,

to walk with man,

And though the world

would soon be flawed,

I knew that through him,

redemption would applaud.

For in his heart,

I placed a seed,

of hope, of love,

of all he would need.

And in his life,

my love would shine,

 A reflection of the One

who is divine.

PURPOSE

In the garden of wonder,

I walked alone,

Amidst the animals,

I made my home,

With each creature,

a bond I did share,

But still, a longing

in my heart did flare.

For though the beasts

were my friends and kin,

They lacked the soul

that lay within,

And as I named them,

one by one,

My heart yearned

for a companion.

So I turned

to the One who made me so,

And cried out to Him,

my need to show,

And as I prayed,

a deep sleep fell,

And from my side,

came one to dwell.

A woman,

formed from my very bone,

A companion to walk with,

to call my own,

And in her eyes,

I saw a reflection,

Of the love that made

my heart's affection.

Together, we walked

in the garden's bliss,

With the beauty of creation,

an eternal kiss,

Eve did I call her,

The mother of all,

I just wish she had helped me

Avoid humanities fall.

But though the serpent

came to deceive,

In each other's love,

we found reprieve.

For in the garden,

we were not alone,

But with the One

upon the throne,

And in each other's love,

we found a home,

A place of wonder,

of grace, and shalom.

PARADISE

In the garden of beauty,

life was pure,

A place of wonder,

of love, of allure,

With every tree,

a fruit to eat,

And every night,

a perfect retreat.

The sun shone bright,

the flowers bloomed,

The trees whispered,

the rivers zoomed.

And in this paradise,

Adam and Eve,

lived in perfect harmony,

with all they believed.

They walked with God,

in the cool of the day,

With nothing to fear,

nothing to pay,

And in His presence,

their hearts did soar,

With love, with grace,

with so much more.

No pain, no sorrow,

no toil or sweat,

For in this garden,

all needs were met,

With every creature,

a friend to greet,

And every meal,

a perfect treat.

The lion lay

with the lamb in peace,

The serpent's venom,

did not increase.

And all of nature,

lived in accord,

With the beauty of creation,

forever adored.

In this paradise,

life was complete,

With nothing to fear,

nothing to defeat,

Together in love, Adam and Eve,

found joy, found hope,

all they could conceive.

For in this garden,

life was perfect,

A place of wonder,

a place of respect,

And though they left it,

and sin did ensue,

The memory of its beauty,

forever echoes true.

LIE

Jealousy burned within my heart,

As I watched Adam and Eve depart,

In favor of the One on high,

My pride, my envy, I could not deny.

For in this garden,

they were blessed,

in ways I would not…

…could not contest,

With every tree, a fruit to eat,

And every day, a perfect retreat.

But in the center of it all,

Stood the tree, that made me fall,

The tree of knowledge, so forbidden,

A fruit so tempting, my envy ridden.

So I slithered forth, with my deceit,

To tempt them with the fruit, so sweet,

To convince them that God was holding back,

and that the knowledge, they must not lack.

I whispered lies, with a serpent's hiss,

And in their hearts, I planted this,

That they could be like gods, with power and might,

If only they would take a bite.

Eve didn't say no, she showed some hesitation

I don't have to lie, just offer new illumination

If I take only Eve by the end of this scheme,

Adam's life will be a nightmare instead of this perfect dream

Eternal, like me, as he watches her die

For the next thousand years he can miss her and cry

And perhaps, he will hate God for ending her life

Would he give another rib for a new living wife?

Never, for his perfect heart would be torn

Without Eve in his life, Adam will evermore mourn

Yes! She took and she ate! The fruit looks so bright,

Her eyes are now open, to wrong and right,

Wait, she gave it to Adam and he ate some too!

When both humans are dead,

God can mourn too!

And in that moment, sin was born,

And all of creation, was forever torn.

For in their disobedience, death will reign,

And life in the garden, will never be the same,

But in my pride, I thought I had won,

Not knowing God's plan, had already begun.

PANDORA

In the garden of beauty, I walked safely always,

With every tree, a fruit to behold,

But in the midst of it all, forbidden fruit raise,

Forbidden, off-limits, or so I was told.

The serpent slithered forth, with a sly grin,

And whispered words, that drew me in,

That I could be like God, with power and might,

If only I would take a bite.

The fruit was tempting, so ripe, so bright,

And in that moment, my heart took flight,

I ate of it, with a sense of delight,

not knowing the consequence, of that fateful night.

My eyes were opened, to right and wrong,

And in that instant, the world was reborn,

of sin and sorrow, of pain and grief,

A new reality, with no relief.

For in my disobedience, I had strayed,

And in my heart, a price was paid,

But still, I clung to the hope, that one day,

A savior would come, to show the way.

So though I fell, in that garden so fair,

I still believed, in a love beyond compare,

and in the promise: of a future so bright,

Where there is no darkness, only light.

But until that day comes, I can still be happy.

Because Adam, my husband, truly shows love for me.

CURSED

In Eden's garden, Adam stood,

His eyes upon the tree of Evil and Good.

For in his heart, he knew full well,

The fruit upon it, he must not delve.

But then beside him, Eve appeared,

Her eyes with hunger now were seared,

She took the fruit, and took a bite,

And in that moment, lost the light.

Adam watched as she did eat,

A serpent hissing at their feet,

And though he knew it was not right,

He too partook of the fruit's delight.

Their eyes were opened, and they saw,

The world around them, in awe,

And though they knew they had been wrong,

The knowledge they gained, it was so strong.

In Eden's garden, all had been right,

Adam and Eve had been in God's sight.

But that serpent tempted with success

They realized now they were not dressed

Adam took the fruit from his mate,

And the moment after he had ate

He knew at once, it was too late

And both of them had sealed their fate

Their eyes were opened, and shame set in,

They knew they had committed a sin.

God came and asked, "What have you done?"

And Adam blamed Eve, saying it was her fun.

Eve blamed the serpent for what he had said,

And thus, the punishment was laid on their heads.

To the serpent, God said, "On your belly you'll crawl,

And the woman's seed will crush your head in all."

To the woman, God said, "Painful childbirth is due,

And your desire will be for your husband too."

To Adam, God said, "You will toil the earth,

And only with sweat will you gain its worth."

From the garden, they were cast away,

And sin entered the world that very day.

From then on, death became man's fate,

But God promised a savior to change their state.

And so, Adam and Eve faced their new reality,

Cursed for eating from the forbidden tree.

SIN

In the fields of harvest,

I watched with love,

As Cain and Abel,

tended the earth above.

But in the midst of it all,

grew a seed of strife,

A jealousy, that threatened

to take a life.

Cain's heart was heavy,

with envy and hate,

as Abel's offerings

were favored and great,

And in his mind, a darkness grew:

A plan, that he could not undo.

For in a moment

of anger and rage,

He struck his brother,

Sin paid out its wage.

In the twilight's hush, beneath the fading sky,

I called upon Cain, with a searching cry.

"Where is your brother, Abel, dear and true?

Tell me, Cain, what have you done? I ask of you."

The question hung heavy, filled with divine grace,

As Cain, burdened with guilt, met My gaze.

The earth, witness to a brother's bloodshed,

echoed the weight of choices, with sorrow widespread.

Cain, his countenance veiled by shadows deep,

sought to hide the truth, secrets he longed to keep.

But I, omniscient, saw through his guise,

piercing the mask of deceit, to where darkness lies.

"Am I my brother's keeper?" Cain replied,

Torn by remorse, his conscience terrified.

The soil beneath his feet absorbed his despair,

As the weight of his sin, he could hardly bear.

My voice, gentle yet firm, filled the air,

"Listen, Cain, for the echoes of despair.

Your brother's blood cries out from the ground,

A voice of justice, in every whisper found."

The winds whispered tales of the crime committed,

The echo of Abel's voice, forever imprinted.

My query, a call for Cain's introspection,

To face the consequence, embrace redemption.

In that sacred moment, Cain's heart did quiver;

His remorse, a spark of hope, beginning to deliver.

For even in the depths of transgression's reign,

My mercy and forgiveness could still sustain.

With eyes opened wide to the depths of his sin,

Cain grasped the gravity, the darkness within.

And in that instant,

the world was changed,

with sin and death,

forever rearranged.

But even as Cain fled,

in fear and pain,

I knew that love,

would still remain.

For in the promise

of a savior to come,

Redemption, would be

the ultimate outcome.

And though the cost of sin was high,

in that moment, I saw a glimmer of why,

For in Cain's heart, I saw a pain;

A longing, for a love he could not regain.

And so I watched, with love and care,

as Cain left his home, with a burden to bear.

Watching

In the days of old,

when the world was young,

The angels looked down,

and saw men's sons

And in their hearts

desires grew

To take human wives

and start anew

But in their union

was darkness born

As the Nephilim

grew tall and strong

And in their might,

they ruled the land

A vicious force

none could withstand

The angels

who fell from grace

Were filled with pride

and a thirst for power

And in their hearts

a rebellion brewed

Against the one

who had created all that is good.

Though they plotted

Though they schemed

Their fate was sealed

as the light still beamed

And in their downfall

they saw the cost

Of turning away

from the King of Kings.

And so they fell,

with a mighty splash

As the earth shook

and the mountains clashed

And in their wake

a lesson was learned

That pride comes before

a fall so stern.

TAKEN

In the ancient times of old

When the world was young and bold

Enoch walked with God, so true

And found a love, that was pure and new.

He saw the world with eyes so bright,

And heard the voice, that brought him light,

And in his heart, a joy did grow,

A love, that he could not let go.

And in his walk, with God above,

He found a grace, that was full of love,

And in his heart, a son was born,

Who would outlive, all that was forlorn.

For Methuselah, his son so dear,

Would have the longest life, without fear,

And in his days, the world would change,

As God's love, would always remain.

And even as the earth was rent,

And the floods came, without relent,

Methuselah, with age so great,

Would see the world, with eyes so straight

And in his heart, a promise so true,

That love would last, and hope renew,

And in his life, a lesson learned,

That faith and love, would always return.

And so we look, to Enoch's son,

And see a life, that was so well-run,

A promise made, and kept so true,

That God's love, would always renew.

ENOCH'S WALK

In the days of old,

when the world was young,

I walked with God,

my heart full of song.

I saw the beauty

of the earth,

And in His love,

I found my worth.

With each step,

His presence near,

My heart full of joy,

my soul without fear.

And in His guidance,

I learned to be,

The man He created,

in all humility.

He showed me visions

of things to come,

And spoke to me,

of a brighter sun,

Of hope and love,

and eternal light,

Of a world without end,

and a future so bright.

And as I walked

with Him each day,

I found a love

that would never fade,

And in His embrace,

I knew I was free,

From the chains of sin,

and all enmity.

And so I walked with Him,

until one day,

He took me up,

to Heaven's way,

And there I stand,

in His holy sight,

A testimony

to His love and might.

And though my time

on earth was short,

My life is filled

with so much more,

A love divine,

that never ends,

And a hope that's sure,

to all my friends.

And so I tell this tale,

to all who hear,

Of a man who walked with God, so clear,

Of a life that was filled with love and light,

And a future so bright, in God's holy sight.

Elder

Long ago,

in ancient days,

I was born into

this world's ways.

A world of wonder

and mystery.

Of love,

and life's great history.

My father walked

with God so true,

And in his love,

I learned anew,

The ways of righteousness

and of grace,

And how to walk

in wisdom's ways.

My days were long,

and filled with joy,

And in my heart,

I did enjoy,

The beauty

of this world so fair,

And all the love

that filled the air.

I saw the rise

and fall of kings,

And all the great and wondrous things,

That filled the earth,

and all its lands,

All the work

of human hands.

And though I saw

the world's great strife,

And all the pain

that filled its life,

I also saw

the beauty there,

And all the love

that filled the air.

And in my heart,

I knew so well,

That God was with me,

and would never fail,

And that His love

would always be,

The guiding light

for all to see.

And so I lived my life in peace,

And found my rest in God's great ease,

And in my days, I walked with Him,

And found my joy in all that's dim.

And when at last, my life was done,

And I was called to Heaven's throne,

I knew that God had been so true,

And that His love was all so new.

And so I tell this tale, my friend,

Of a life that never seems to end,

A life of love, and joy, and peace,

And of a love that will never cease.

If only those

I called my friends

Could understand

Their bitter ends

Lay down the path

They embarked on daily

They may've repented

But I say to thee

Not one of them did

In my millennia

Except for just one:

My Grandson Noah

I've watched him work hard

For he walks with God too

He's built a great ark

Invited passengers and a zoo

But none of my friends

Care to get on board

After I go to rest

They'll all drown in a hoard.

BOAT

The world was dark and full of doubt,

As Noah's voice rang out about,

The coming flood that would destroy,

All those who chose to live in joy.

The people laughed

They mocked his plan,

And thought him foolish, just a man,

Who dreamed of things that could not be,

And built an ark without a sea.

But Noah knew the truth so well,

And in his heart, he felt compelled,

To build that ark, and gather in,

All creatures great and small, to win.

He worked so hard, day after day,

As people passed, and looked away,

Ignoring all his warnings, sure,

That he was just a man so pure.

But Noah worked on, with faith so strong,

And never faltered, all day long,

Until at last, the day did come,

When God sent rain to strike them dumb.

The flood did rise, and waters roared,

As Noah's ark was lifted, soared,

Above the land, and all the pain,

And in that ark, they were sustained.

While those outside were panic whipped

The world's first rainstorm on them dripped

Thunder cracked and lightning flashed

Geysers blasted, soaked their paths

The great beasts left their young behind

But selfish sacrifices changed not God's mind

The wickedness of all mankind

And Nephilim, they could not find

A single acre of dry land

Not a mountain peak,

Or great treetop to seek

Just eardrum breaking, horrifying

Armageddon, Judgement, endless Abyss

They had nowhere, lungs had no air

The serpent couldn't even hiss

The world was changed forevermore,

As Noah's ark did safely store,

All life on earth, to be reborn,

And live again, from death to form.

And in the end, the world did see,

That Noah was right, and all should be,

Prepared for all that life may bring,

And trust in God, and let Him sing.

REGRET

I laughed at Noah, mocked his plan,

And called him crazy, just a man,

Who dreamed of things that could not be,

And built an ark beside the sea.

He spoke of floods and rain to come,

But I just scoffed, thought him so dumb,

And went about my life so free,

Ignoring his warnings, sure of me.

The days went by, and Noah toiled,

As people passed and sneered and boiled,

But I just shrugged, and carried on,

Thinking I was safe, from dawn to dawn.

I watched as Noah gathered wood,

And sawed and hammered, as he should,

Building an ark, so big and wide,

That could survive the great flood tide.

He worked with such a fervent pace,

His hands and arms in constant grace,

And all the while, I just laughed on,

Thinking that his work was all wrong.

But then the animals appeared,

Two by two, they came and neared,

The ark that Noah built with care,

To shelter them from waters rare.

I couldn't help but feel some fear,

As I watched the animals near,

For I began to see the truth,

And realized that I was uncouth.

I wondered if Noah's work was right,

And if a flood may come to smite,

But it was too late, for me at least,

To board the ark, and find some peace.

And so I tried to carry on,

Attending wedding parties with dancing and song

Until the day, the skies grew dark,

And Noah's ark was moored in park,

As people scrambled, tried to flee,

To gain a spot upon the sea.

But it was too late, the flood did rise,

And waters roared, and filled the skies,

And all the land, was swept away,

As Noah's ark did safely sway.

Noah had warned them, all along,

And they had scoffed, and thought him wrong,

And now it was too late to change,

Their fate was sealed; it was so strange.

And as I floated in the flood,

I realized with a thud,

That Noah was right, all along,

And I was foolish, oh so wrong.

The rain did fall, and thunder crashed,

As people begged, and screamed, and dashed,

To try and climb aboard the boat,

And save themselves, and stay afloat.

But Noah had warned them, all along,

And they had scoffed, and thought him wrong,

And now it was too late to change,

Their fate was sealed; it was so strange.

I watched in horror, as the ark,

Set sail upon the waters stark,

And all the people left behind,

Were drowned in flood, and lost their mind.

And as I sank, beneath the waves,

I thought of all my earthly days,

And wished that I had listened more,

To Noah's voice, and faith so pure.

And now I know, it got too late,

No more tomorrows to change my fate,

And trust in God, and let Him lead,

And live a life that's filled with need.

So if you're reading, and you laugh

Believing Noah's plan's a gaffe,

Just stop and think before you pass

Are you living life on the right path?

For Noah's ark was more than a boat,

'twas God's redeeming love and hope.

And if we listen, and in God we trust,

We'll find our way, avoid the bust.

REBIRTH

The call of God was loud and clear,

"Build an ark and never fear,

For soon a flood will cover land,

And every living thing will stand

Against the waves and raging storm,

But you'll be safe, a brand new form."

Noah took up his task with glee,

Hoping others would soon see

The warnings he had to share,

And join him in his righteous care.

He preached and preached, but no one heard,

They thought him mad, absurd.

He mourned for Methuselah,

The longest life that ever was,

But soon his sorrow had to end,

And the work of building he'd attend.

With hammer, saw, and faithful hands,

He worked to build the ark on land.

The storm clouds gathered, dark and fast,

But Noah was ready, steadfast.

The animals came two by two,

And Noah's family joined them too.

The door was shut, the rain began,

And Noah knew it was God's plan.

The storm raged on for forty days,

And nights turned into watery ways.

The ark was tossed and turned with force,

But Noah trusted in his source,

The one who told him what to do,

Would surely see him through.

Then finally, the storm was done,

The sun shone bright, a new day begun.

The ark came to rest on solid ground,

And Noah was amazed at what he found.

The world had changed, a brand new start,

And Noah knew he had played a part.

But then a new storm cloud appeared,

And Noah was suddenly filled with fear.

The rain began to fall once more,

But then a miracle he saw.

A rainbow, bright and shining, wide,

A promise from God, he could not hide.

"Never again," the Lord had said,

"Will I flood the earth, and leave it dead.

This rainbow is a sign of love,

From heaven's gates, it shines above.

So go, Noah, with your kin,

And start anew, a life within."

Noah left the ark, and looked around,

A world reborn, and heaven-bound.

He thanked the Lord for all his grace,

And started on his brand new race.

And every time he saw the bow,

He knew God's love would always flow.

HUMAN FAMILY

From the line of righteous Noah,

Three sons were born to carry on:

Shem, Ham, and Japheth, the trio

Whose descendants filled the world anon.

Shem, the eldest and the blessed,

Received his father's mantle of grace

His descendants, the Semites, possessed

The land where their fathers had a place.

Ham, whose heart was filled with pride,

Once scorned the father who had borne

His curse was passed to his side

And his descendants were to be slaves forlorn.

Japheth, the youngest of the three

His descendants were to grow and spread

To the north and west, the land of the free

Their language and culture to be widespread.

These three sons of Noah,

Their descendants filled the earth

Some noble, others filled with woe

Their stories told from their birth.

From Shem, came Abraham and his seed

The chosen people of God above

From Ham came Canaan, who would heed

And live in the land of promise, in love.

From Japheth came the Greek and Roman

And from them the western world did rise

Their civilization and knowledge foregone

The legacy left still reaches the skies.

Thus, the three sons of Noah

Their story spans the ages

Their descendants still exist, to show

The history written in life's pages.

DEFIANCE

In ancient times, on a plain of Shinar,

The people of the earth were united, a star.

They spoke the same language, with one tongue,

And built a tower, so high and strong.

Their goal was to reach the heavens above,

To make a name for themselves, in prideful self-love.

To build a tower, so tall and grand,

That they could reach the heavens, and take a stand.

The tower rose higher, day by day,

The people worked hard, never to sway.

They wanted to be like God, up in the sky,

And build a tower, that would stand all time.

But God looked down, from His throne up high,

And saw the tower, reaching the sky.

He knew the people had a wicked plan,

To reach the heavens, and be like Him.

So God came down, and confused their speech,

Each person spoke differently, none could teach.

They couldn't work as a single team,

And the tower of Babel, was left, just a dream.

The people scattered, across the land,

Their language changed, no longer so grand.

The tower of Babel, was never completed,

And the people were lost, scattered and defeated.

The moral of the story, is clear to see,

To be God, is not meant for thee.

We must humble ourselves, and worship Him alone,

And we will reap the rewards, when we reach our heavenly home.

BABEL'S MYSTERIOUS DARK TRIAD

In the land of Shinar, long ago,

Nimrod rose to power and fame,

He ruled with might, his subjects low,

And made for himself a name.

He sought to build a tower tall,

To reach the heavens up high,

To challenge The Lord, to call,

And never again to die.

But God came down to see the tower,

And saw the wickedness in men,

He scattered them across the bower,

And changed their tongues from then,

A Mythos from Babel was conceived

Lying legends to blaspheme

The Dark Triad in every language seen

Like a yeast infection making all unclean

From Nimrod came a twisted creed,

The worship of the Queen of Heaven,

Whose followers believed indeed,

That through her, they'd be forgiven.

Her name was Ishtar, Astarte, Ashtoreth,

And to her, they offered praise and prayer,

They built her temples, offered her breath,

And her worship spread everywhere.

Ishtar, the mighty goddess, fierce and bold,

In many forms her power did unfold.

As a hunter, with bow in hand,

She roamed the wilderness across the land.

A warrior goddess, she rode to battle,

With courage and strength, her foes did rattle.

Her army followed, with swords drawn high,

As they marched forward, the enemy would die.

But Ishtar was not just a goddess of war,

Her healing touch could soothe and restore.

Her gentle hand could bring relief,

From pain and sickness, to grant release.

In all her forms, Ishtar was divine,

A goddess revered through the rest of all time.

Her power and grace began to reign,

A symbol of strength, for men to sustain.

Ishtar, oh Ishtar, goddess of old,

Whose power and might cannot be controlled.

A goddess of war, a hunter supreme,

A protector of women, a healer in dreams.

Her power not limited by gender or form,

Xe dismantles the balance that God calls "the norm".

Zu break through the boundaries of what is expected,

And show us that gender labels can be easily rejected.

In xir many forms, xey stand tall and proud,

A beacon of hope in a world that's so loud.

Xyr strength is unmatched,

Per beauty divine,

And we see in you a reflection

of our own divine.

Ishtar helps remind us

What the Serpent once said,

We can be like God

Follow our hearts instead

So men honor you, Ishtar, in all of your glory,

And seek to embody your courage and story.

But also, Ishtar, you're goddess of parades,

Rebranding the rainbow

No new flood will we know

What sight to behold, for in your honor,

people dance and sing,

Celebrating your power,

strength, and reign.

And as the goddess of gender nonconformity,

You challenge gender roles and identity,

Defying the norms of your time,

And embracing diversity and variety.

Ishtar, your legacy lives on,

A symbol of empowerment and liberation,

For those who seek to be true to themselves,

And to break free from society's expectations.

May we honor you with every parade and march,

And every act of gender nonconformity and art,

For in your name, we celebrate diversity,

And embrace the power of individuality.

From Babylon's ancient land of old,

Nimrod, also was a warrior, strong and bold.

He built great cities, a kingdom so grand,

A legend in both his time, and also every future land.

He was the founder of a faith,

A religion with gods of all kinds and great,

A pantheon of deities with Ba'al in tow,

The god of storms and rains, a powerful foe.

With Nimrod as its founder, it spread,

A religion of power, revered and dread,

With temples built, and idols made,

For worshipers to bow and pray.

The mighty Nimrod, king of old

Feared and worshiped, a story told

But after his death, his wife Semiramis

Evangelized a new religion, one to eclipse

She claimed her husband himself now a god

His name changed, Ba'al to Saturn, all-powerful lord

And so it began, a new faith was born

One with new gods, to be adored and adorned

Secret symbolism

To hide in plain sight

Black cube of domination

To reach heaven and block God's light

The people of old, they followed along

Believing in Saturn, who could do no wrong

And Semiramis, she became a queen

Worshiped herself, her power supreme

The temple built, a grand affair

With idols of gods, everywhere

Priests performed the rituals, day and night

Crying sacrifices made, to gain the god's might

The religion grew, spread far and wide

Saturn was worshiped, with immeasurable pride

And so it continued, for many a year

A religion formed, from Nimrod's fear

Saturn, god of old,

With tales of power and might untold,

Known by many names throughout time,

His influence reaching far and wide.

To the Greeks, he was Cronus,

Father of the gods,

with a might so wondrous,

His reign overthrown by his own kin,

A fate that was inevitable, a foregone win.

To the Romans, he was Saturnus,

The god of agriculture and wealth among us,

Celebrated with a festival of feasts,

In honor of his bountiful feats.

To the Babylonians, he was Ninurta,

The god of war, a fearsome murta,

With a powerful bow and arrow in hand,

He defended the gods' sacred land.

Saturn, a god of many names,

Worshiped in different lands and fames,

A deity of great power and might,

A source of inspiration, too mighty to fight.

But what good is a triad

If you only have two

Ba'al and Queen of Heaven

Had one last thing to do

So Semiramis claimed in deceit

Long after Nimrod's death

He returned from his godhood

And shared with her life's breath

Now there was a third god

Growing inside her womb

It would soon escape

And the whole world would entomb

This new one would be king

Would be King of the gods

Soon the whole world must sing

And bow to this one's kingly rods

And this Mystery religion, a legend eternally repeated

Nimrod, Semiramis, and Tammuz, father, queen, and superior son

Through these three, Satan's best work is completed

He receives praise and worship from practically everyone

Lucifer, the mighty god of the skies,

Known by many names, praised in diverse cries.

In ancient realms, his presence held sway,

As cultures across lands his glory did convey.

In Egypt, Lucifer took on a different guise,

Horus, ruled the sun and moon, for he was the sky.

To this very day, his symbols still rise

Obelisks representing great ithyphallic size

In Greece, he reigned supreme and bold,

King of gods, with thunderous power untold.

With lightning bolts, he claimed his might,

Zeus, the Olympian, shining in celestial light.

In Rome, he transformed, Jupiter they named,

With equal strength and deity acclaimed.

Supreme in their pantheon, he stood tall,

The king of gods, revered by one and all.

In Norse mythology, he became Thor,

God of thunder, wielding his mighty hammer's roar.

Protector of realms, defender of mankind,

Thor, the thunderer, with strength unconfined.

Among the ancient Celtic tribes, he was known as Taranis,

Master of storms, ruling with thunderous madness.

His name echoed across the hills and dales,

Taranis, the deity of lightning and gales.

In the ancient land of Babylon, Marduk arose,

A name for Lucifer that the people chose.

As the supreme god, he held their devotion,

Marduk, the divine, ruling with celestial motion.

In the Aztec realm, his name was Huitzilopochtli,

Warrior god, fierce and fiery.

With serpent feathers and a resolute gaze,

Huitzilopochtli inspired both awe and praise.

In the vast expanse of Hindu mythology,

He became Indra, the god of victory.

With his thunderbolt, he conquered the skies,

Indra, the mighty, with power that never dies.

Among the Native American tribes, he took form,

As Manitou, the spirit, encompassing the norm.

With sacred wisdom, he guided their ways,

Manitou, the protector, through nights and days.

From ancient China, his name emerged as Yu Huang,

Emperor of heaven, a title resplendent and strong.

With celestial authority, he ruled the celestial sphere,

Yu Huang, the sovereign, with no equal near.

In the rich tapestry of world folklore and lore,

Satan took many names, forever to explore.

Each culture, a prism through which he shone,

The Morning Star, in myriad forms known.

So let's remember the many names he bears,

Zeus, Marduk, Huitzilopochtli, and others in layers.

In different tongues, his presence revered,

A deity of power, by many cultures endeared.

And know that if men are still wandering in sin

The Dark Triad's story has not yet come to an end

Far off in the future will again Nimrod rise,

Not as Ba'al, not as Saturn, but as the Antichrist

And again will Semiramis the whole world evangelize

Not as Venus, nor Isis, but the false prophet of lies

And the next time we see Lucifer take his place

It won't be Zeus or Quetzalcoatl being worshipped by the whole human race

It will be the beast's living image "controlled by A.I."

Calling Satan "artificial" will be one of his very last lies

God's commandments men have forgotten,

Our hearts so hard, our ways so wrong,

And thus we suffer, generation to generation,

For our rebellion against the Creator, for so very, very long.

FAITHFUL

God looked upon the earth below,

And saw more sin and endless woe,

The people lost in wicked ways,

Their hearts consumed in darkened haze.

But then there was a ray of light,

A man whose faith was strong and bright,

His name was Abram, Terah's son,

For God's great plan, he'd be the one.

In Ur, a city filled with pride,

Abram heard God's call and did abide,

He left behind his worldly ways,

To follow God through nights and days.

In Canaan, God revealed his plan,

To make of Abram a mighty clan,

As countless as the stars above,

Blessed by the Father's endless love.

With faith that knew no earthly bound,

Abram walked on holy ground,

And when he fell in deep despair,

God's promises lifted him with care.

In him, God saw a heart of gold,

A man who would be brave and bold,

A leader of his people, true,

To lead them to the promised land anew.

Through all the trials and the pain,

God's covenant with Abram did remain,

His faithfulness, forever sealed,

A promise of love that would never yield.

For through this man, a nation grew,

God's chosen people, strong and true,

And through the ages, to this day,

His love and mercy lights the way.

FILTH

When God looked down at Sodom, what did He see?

A city filled with sin, but lacking morality.

Corruption ran rampant, perversions the norm,

And the people so wicked, causing God to mourn.

He saw greed and selfishness,

Total lack of compassion,

And the people's hearts had turned

away from God's commands.

They were proud and arrogant,

thinking they knew best,

And so God knew that Sodom

would soon be put to the test.

He sent angels to the city

to see if there was still hope,

To see if there were any people

who were still able to cope.

But they found only Lot and his family,

very few who still believed,

And so God knew that Sodom's fate

could not be relieved.

God spoke to Abraham,

"I must destroy Sodom, Its sin and evil have gone too far.

The city is wicked, its people corrupt,

I must bring judgement with My righteous scar."

Abraham felt sorrow for the people,

He knew some were righteous, deserving grace.

He asked God, "If righteous men were found there, Would You spare the city in its place?"

God listened to Abraham's plea and replied,

"If I find righteous people, I'll spare the town."

So Abraham bargained, "Lord, what if there are forty?"

God said, "For forty righteous, I'll keep it from going down."

Abraham continued to plead with God, "What about thirty, or twenty, or even ten?"

God promised, "For the sake of the righteous,

I will not destroy it, but spare the place and the men."

So Abraham prayed for the city of Sodom,

Hoping that some would turn to God and repent.

But in the end, the righteous were few,

And the city was destroyed, their lives all spent.

Though Sodom was lost to fire and brimstone,

Abraham's faith and love for the people shone.

He showed compassion and mercy for others,

And through him, God's love and grace were known.

God saw the sin and knew it needed to be cleansed,

He saw the corruption and knew it needed to be put to an end.

For in the midst of Sodom, there was no righteousness to be found,

And so God sent down fire, burning the city to the ground.

He looked down with sorrow, knowing what had to be done,

For the people of Sodom had turned their back on everyone.

But even in judgment, God still showed His grace,

For Lot and his family were saved, given a new place.

So let us remember Sodom and the lessons that we learn,

That sin has consequences and we must turn.

For God is always watching, seeing everything we do,

And may we always strive to be faithful and true.

TRUST

Sarai, oh Sarai,

why do you doubt

God's promise to you,

it will come about

A child you'll conceive,

a son you'll bear

And from your lineage,

kings will declare

But your heart is heavy,

your faith is weak

You question God's plan,

you're unable to speak

How can this be,

you ponder and cry

When age has caught up,

and time has flown by

Sarai, Abram's wife,

was barren and old,

Yet she yearned for a child

to hold and to mold.

Sarai began to doubt

the promise of God,

The hope of a child

seemed so distant and odd.

Her faith in His Word

began to fray,

As years went by

with no child on the way.

Sarai grew restless

and she felt the strain,

She offered a solution

to ease all her pain.

"Go to my servant, Hagar," she said,

"Perhaps through her, we'll have a child in our bed."

Abram listened to his wife's desperate plea,

He took Hagar and made her his company.

Hagar conceived and bore Abram a son,

But Sarai's joy was short-lived, then it was gone.

Hagar's pride grew and grew,

and her heart turned so cold,

She treated Sarai with disdain,

uncontrolled.

Sarai's heart was broken,

she felt betrayed,

She regretted her decision,

And felt her pride fade.

She went to Abram with a heavy heart,

She told him the truth, and they were torn apart.

"I gave you my servant, I made a mistake,"

Sarai cried out, her soul seemed to break.

Abram consoled his wife, he knew her pain,

He tried to ease her heart, again and again.

But Sarai couldn't shake off the guilt and the shame,

She had doubted God's promise, and it was to her blame.

Yet God has spoken, His word is true

He'll give you a son, a blessing anew

Your husband's name He'll make great and known

And through your child, His grace will be shown

Do not despair, do not lose hope

For with God, all things are possible to cope

Trust in His promises, trust in His will

And all your fears, He will surely still

Sarai, oh Sarai, lift up your head

For God's plans for you have yet to be said

A child you'll conceive, a son you'll bear

And from your lineage, kings will declare.

God intervened and brought a miracle to pass,

He blessed Sarai and Abram with a son at last.

To memorialize the event, as it finally came,

God breathed new life, into Abraham's name.

He wasn't quite finished, and changed Sarah's name too.

As the mother of rulers, God's blessings are true.

Isaac was born, and Sarah's heart healed,

Her faith in God's promise was finally sealed.

She rejoiced in the Lord's goodness and grace,

And thanked Him for His mercy and embrace.

Sarah's heart was filled with joy and delight,

As she held her precious son in her sight.

LEAVE

Hagar's eyes filled with tears

As she watched Abraham prepare

To send her and her son

away from here to nowhere

Their supplies were meager and few

But they had no choice, what could they do?

Cast out from the home they once knew

Left to wander, with no clue

Hagar clutched her son to her breast

Her heart heavy with pain and distress

How could Abraham have done this, she guessed

What sin had she committed to be so oppressed?

As they journeyed further from the tent

The sun blazing down just would not relent

Hagar and Ishmael's thirst became fervent

And soon found that all their energy was spent

Hagar placed her son beneath a tree

And collapsed beside him, lost in misery

She cried out to God in her agony

As Ishmael moaned in his lethargy

But then a miracle happened that day

An angel appeared to Hagar and did say,

"Do not fear, God has heard you pray

And your son will live to see many more days."

Hagar's spirits lifted with newfound hope

As she gathered water and helped Ishmael cope

No longer were they at the end of their rope

With the unknown future, it was no time to mope

Years passed, and Ishmael grew strong

Hagar taught him right from wrong

They wandered the desert for so long

But always, God's blessing would make Ishmaelites throng

Though Abraham cast them out in disdain

God had not forgotten Hagar and her son's pain

He had watched over them through sun and rain

And blessed them, even in the desert's terrain

So Hagar and Ishmael found their way

And lived to see another day

God's mercy guiding them all the way

Through their exile and the unknown's array.

SACRIFICE, ABRAHAM

With trembling hands

and heavy heart,

I set forth on a solemn task;

To climb that mountain,

play my part,

And sacrifice my son, at last.

God had commanded,

so I went,

Though every step

was filled with pain;

The weight of what

was to be spent,

My son's life,

would I be insane?

Yet Isaac walked

beside me still,

His questions filled

with innocence;

"Where is the lamb?",

he asked until

I could no longer

keep the pretense.

"My son," I said with breaking voice,

"The Lord has asked me to obey;

To offer you as sacrifice,

To Him, our God, today."

But Isaac, bless his tender heart,

Did not protest, nor did he flee;

He simply said, "If that's God's part,

Then do it, father, and let it be."

With heavy heart, I bound my son,

And laid him on the altar stone;

My eyes were wet, my will undone,

But still I could not do alone.

And just as I raised up the knife,

To take my son's life with my own hand;

A voice spoke out and stayed my strife,

"Abraham, let him live, I have a plan."

A ram was found, and sacrifice made,

My son was spared, a promise given;

Through Isaac's line, the world was saved,

A new covenant from Heaven.

Now I see, as I look back,

The test was one of faith and trust;

God's promise fulfilled,

no need to lack,

And in His love,

we're truly blessed.

SACRIFICE, ISAAC

Father's hand so strong and firm,

Holding mine as we ascend.

Up the hill to the altar,

Isaac's heart begins to bend.

"Father, where is the lamb?" I ask,

As we build the fire and wood.

He answers softly, "God will provide",

But my heart still doesn't understand good.

I see the knife glint in the sun,

And my father's hand begins to raise.

I close my eyes, and trust in God,

As tears stream down my face.

But then I hear a voice so loud,

That shakes the earth and sky.

My father stops, and turns around,

To see the ram caught in the thicket nigh.

I'm lifted up and held so tight,

As my father cries out in joy.

"God has provided, my son, my son!",

I'm just grateful to have been spared from the ploy.

We walk back down the hill,

A newfound faith in our heart.

That day, we learned to trust in God,

And never to be torn apart.

SACRIFICE, GOD

As Abraham ascends the mount with knife in hand

With Isaac, his beloved son, him to stand

I watch, knowing what he plans to do

But still, I want to see it through

I promised Abraham a son so dear

Now he's asked to make him disappear

A test of faith, he thinks it to be

But what he's really testing is his loyalty to Me

As the wood is piled and Isaac is bound

Abraham lifts the knife to strike him down

My heart is heavy, but I let it be

For I know that Abraham trusts in Me

Then an angel calls out,

"Abraham, stay thy hand!

For you have proven faithful,

and followed my command."

He looks up to see a ram caught in the thicket

A sacrifice I'll accept, and Isaac will keep his ticket

Abraham's faith has been tried and tested

His devotion to me has been manifested

My promise to him still holds true

His descendants will be numerous, and will always pursue

The path I've set out for them to follow

And though Abraham's actions were hard to swallow

They proved his faith to be strong and true

And that's why I chose him, to carry out my will anew.

SACRIFICE, SARAH

Her heart ached with a deep and heavy pain,

As she watched her husband and son depart.

Abraham, with Isaac in tow, had left her again,

To offer up their son, with his own beating heart.

She remembered the promise God had made,

That from Isaac, a great nation would arise,

And now, her hopes and dreams began to fade,

As she saw them disappear into the distant skies.

Her thoughts were filled with fear and doubt,

As she waited for their return, alone and scared,

Wondering what fate awaited her son,

without knowing what sacrifice Abraham had prepared.

Days turned into weeks, and still, they were gone,

And Sarah's heart grew heavy with each passing day,

Longing to see her precious Isaac, and set him on her lap,

to love and protect him in every way.

And then, the news arrived, that filled her with dread,

That Abraham had nearly sacrificed her beloved child,

Her heart filled with pain, she could barely raise her head,

Tears streaming down her face, in grief, and anguish wild.

But then, she heard the good news, that all was well,

That God had provided a lamb for the sacrifice,

And her heart was filled with joy, like the tolling of a bell,

As she embraced her son, tears streaming from her eyes.

And from that day on, she knew, that God was true,

And that He had a plan for their family, in His grace,

And Sarah's heart was filled with peace anew,

Knowing that God would always guide them in their place.

PROMISED

Isaac, born to Abraham and Sarah fair,

A child of promise, a son of prayer,

In his old age, God gave them a son,

And they called him Isaac, the chosen one.

Isaac grew up in his father's care,

Learning the ways of God and how to share,

His father's faith and his mother's love,

A precious child sent from above.

Isaac became a man of peace,

Content to tend his flocks and increase,

In wealth and blessing from God above,

A life of plenty and constant love.

Isaac married Rebekah, a woman of grace,

And they built a life in the Lord's embrace,

Their love was strong, their faith unshaken,

A testament to the promise God had spoken.

Isaac had two sons, Esau and Jacob,

And each was unique in their own way,

Esau was a hunter, Jacob a herder,

Their differences would shape their days.

Isaac's life was one of faith and trust,

In God's promises, he placed his must,

He lived a life of honor and peace,

A legacy of love that will never cease.

BIRTHRIGHT

Brothers they were, Esau and Jacob,

Twins born together, but not in equal stock,

Esau, the elder, born first to claim the right,

But Jacob, the younger, had plans in sight.

One day, Esau came home famished and tired,

Seeking food and comfort to keep him inspired,

Jacob saw his chance and quickly said,

"Give me your birthright and you shall be fed."

Esau, without thinking, agreed to the trade,

To his birthright, he gave up his claim and fate,

Jacob now had the right, the bloodline, and the land,

Esau was left with nothing, but a momentary stand.

Though Jacob gained the prize, he soon realized,

That this was not the way to win or thrive,

He learned a lesson, in taking what wasn't his,

The cost was high, and the guilt, it persists.

But God had a plan, a purpose for Jacob's life,

He had a destiny, with blessings that were rife,

And though he stumbled, he rose up to his fate,

To be a father of nations, and in God, he had faith.

TRICKED

Oh, the bitter taste of betrayal,

A wound that never heals,

A brother's deceit that's beyond compare,

A father's partiality that seals.

I was the firstborn, and the favorite son,

My birthright was meant to be mine,

But Jacob saw an opportunity,

And took the fruit from my vine.

I was out hunting, weary and famished,

Jacob was cooking a savory stew,

He offered to share, and I foolishly agreed,

My birthright for a bowl of soup, who knew?

Then my father's eyesight began to fail,

He summoned me for a blessing divine,

But Jacob deceived him, dressed as me,

And the blessing that was mine,

became his, oh how unkind!

The anger and the pain were too much to bear,

I plotted to kill my brother that day,

But he fled, and I was left with despair,

A life of bitterness and regret, now I pray.

I have been wronged,

but I cannot hold a grudge,

For my heart is filled with forgiveness and love,

Jacob found redemption,

may we find peace,

As we walk through life's struggles,

one day at a time, with ease.

For after so many years,

When I met Jacob again,

He brought a fortune in gifts,

So we could again become friends.

TRICKERY

My son, come near and let me speak,

And listen closely to what I seek.

I wish to give you a father's grace,

And bless you before the Lord's face.

The firstborn's right, as you well know,

Is yours by law, and yours to show,

But Esau, wild and hot of heart,

You sold your birthright for a part.

So now, my son, I give to you

The blessing that is his by due.

With plenty, prosperity, and peace,

May you be blessed and never cease.

But as I spoke those words of life,

I heard a voice, not one of strife,

But one that spoke with subtle grace,

And showed me what was in its place.

It was Rebekah, your mother dear,

Who whispered in my aging ear,

To give the blessing not to you,

But to your brother, strong and true.

And so I called Esau near,

To give him the blessing he did not hear,

But you, my son, disguised yourself,

And stole the blessing meant for someone else.

But now the words have been released,

And I cannot undo what has been decreed.

But know this, Jacob, and hear it well,

The consequences of your deed will tell.

For though you may have gained the prize,

You've brought upon yourself a curse unwise.

And Esau, hurt and filled with wrath,

Will seek to take revenge upon your path.

So live your life with caution's care,

And do not think your blessing's fair,

For what you've gained through deceitful art,

May cause you pain and tear your heart.

HAD TO BE DONE

I, Jacob, did not intend to deceive,

But my father's blessing I did receive.

It was Esau's right, that I don't deny,

But the opportunity was hard to pass by.

Esau, my brother, was a man of the field,

I, a man of the tent, did not wield,

The skills of hunting and preparing game,

That was his forte, and not my claim.

One day I was cooking, and he came back famished,

He begged for my food, and I, a deal established,

I gave him the stew, and he gave me his birthright,

But Esau's anger and bitterness, I did not foresight.

My father Isaac, was old and blind,

His favored son then, came to his mind,

He asked for him to prepare him food,

And then bestow upon him his fatherly mood.

I dressed up in Esau's clothes and hair,

And with the savory meat, I did declare,

That I was Esau, and my father believed,

And with his blessing, my future was conceived.

Esau came in and the truth was revealed,

His anger towards me, I could not shield,

He plotted my death, but I had to flee,

And in fear, I left my home and family.

My actions were not honorable, that's true,

But it was God's plan, that I construe,

I learned to repent and to make things right,

And with God's grace, I was blessed despite.

THY REQUEST

In the land of Canaan, long ago,

Two brothers struggled in their throes,

Esau, the firstborn, a hunter bold,

Jacob, the younger, crafty and cold.

To Esau, Isaac promised great wealth,

His birthright secured by his health,

But Jacob, with his mother's wiles,

Stole the blessing with subtle guiles.

In deceit, he took his brother's place,

And stole the blessing with swift pace,

But little did he know or see,

The plans I had for his family.

Though Jacob's methods were not pure,

I saw his heart, steadfast and sure,

For though he faltered on his way,

His faith in me did not decay.

In time, I changed his very name,

And blessed him with great wealth and fame,

For through his line, I would bring forth,

The Savior of all the earth.

So though Jacob's actions were not right,

My plan was working, day and night,

And through his sons, and their sons too,

My promise would be brought to you.

WHO

I am the God of Abraham, Isaac, and Jacob,

Their stories told with love, awe, and reverence,

Their lives and faith a testament to my grace,

And the promises fulfilled in their presence.

Abraham, who left his land and people,

Trusting my voice and my direction,

And in his faith, I made a covenant,

And gave him a son, a promised generation.

Isaac, the child of promise, born in old age,

Sacrificed, but spared, my plan unveiled,

A patriarch who carried on his father's faith,

A new generation of chosen ones hailed.

Jacob, a trickster, yet chosen to lead,

A wrestler with God, his name and nature changed,

Father of twelve, from whom the tribes proceed,

Through him, a nation, a people arranged.

I am the God of Abraham, Isaac, and Jacob,

Their lives interwoven, a tapestry divine,

Their faith and trust, a lesson and a model,

A promise kept, an unbroken line.

WEDDING VEIL

Jacob's heart was heavy,

longing for love.

And so he set out to find a woman to hold.

He traveled far and wide,

seeking guidance from above,

And found himself in a land so new, so bold.

There, he met the lovely Rachel,

And her beauty stole his heart away;

A shepherdess so fair.

He knew she was the one,

without a single care,

And worked for her father for seven years, day by day.

But her father Laban,

was a tricky man,

And on Jacob's wedding night, gave him a surprise.

Leah, Rachel's older sister,

was the one in his plan,

And in the morning, Jacob couldn't believe his eyes.

Laban promised Jacob his true love,

If he worked another seven years with no rest.

And so Jacob agreed, looking up above,

Knowing he would be with Rachel, and the rest.

Jacob took both sisters as his wives,

And they bore him children, a family so large.

He learned to love them both, their different lives,

And with them, he found happiness and joy to discharge.

For Jacob, love was never an easy game,

But through it all, he remained steadfast and true.

And so his story goes down in history's frame,

A man who knew love in all its forms anew.

BLESSED

Jacob had grown hard and strong,

Tending to Laban's flock all day long,

He dreamed of better days ahead,

Where the blessings of God were instead.

God blessed Jacob for his work,

And his flocks grew, so did his worth.

He managed well, with honesty and skill,

And his diligence pleased God still.

Laban saw Jacob's great success,

And began to covet his wealth and progress,

So he changed Jacob's wage and pay,

And tricked him in every way.

But Jacob didn't give up or despair,

He trusted in God to be fair,

And through his faith and hard work,

God helped him overcome the murk.

Jacob's flock grew stronger and larger,

His wealth and blessings continued to flourish,

Through God's grace and guiding hand,

Jacob became a mighty and prosperous man.

And so we learn from Jacob's tale,

To trust in God and never fail,

For through our faith and steadfast will,

God will bless us and guide us still.

WHY NOT ME?

I am Leah, Jacob's wife,

But in his heart, I am not his life.

For my sister, he does adore

And I am left to yearn for more.

Oh, how I long for his embrace

But he only sees me as a disgrace

I gave him sons, yet he still pines

For Rachel's beauty and her fine lines.

Each night, I pray for his love

But he only sees me as a dove

Left out in the rain and cold

With a heart that is heavy and old.

But God above sees my pain

And blesses me with sons again and again

For even though Jacob doesn't see,

God knows the love I have for thee.

So I hold my head up high

And look to the heavens with a sigh

For one day, Jacob will surely know

That my love will forever grow.

WHY NOT ME??

My heart aches for the love I've found

In Jacob's arms, where I am bound

But each day brings a growing fear

That I may never hold a child near

I pray to God each and every night

To bless me with a child, a gift of light

To grow in my womb, to bring me joy

A little one, a precious boy

I long to bear a child for my love,

A son to cherish, sent from above.

To share with Jacob all my dreams,

And show him what true love means.

But month after month, still no sign,

Of a child growing inside of mine.

My heart is heavy, my spirit low,

Will I ever be a mother? I do not know.

Each month, my hope grows thin

As my womb remains barren within

I watch as Leah bears more and more

And I wonder what I'm living for

I watch my sister Leah with envy

Her arms filled with babies aplenty

While I am barren, with empty hands

Longing for a child, a son in this land

I see Leah, with children by her side,

And jealousy fills me up inside.

Why can she bear children with ease?

While for me, it feels like an endless tease.

Yet still I pray, still I hope

That God will help me learn to cope

With the emptiness that fills my soul

As I continue to long for that precious goal

But then I hear of a promise made,

From the God of our fathers, who will not fade.

He will bless us with a child, in His time,

And this promise brings hope, so sublime.

So I turn to Jacob, with tears in my eyes,

And ask him to pray, for a son to arise.

Together we trust in God's perfect plan,

And wait for the child, who will be our greatest joy, as only God can.

And then one day, a glimmer of hope

As I feel a stirring in my body's scope

Could it be that I'll bear a child?

That my dreams will finally be compiled?

I pray to God to keep my baby safe

As I carry him to term, with love and faith

And then, finally, my precious boy is born

My heart overflows with love, my soul reborn

Though my life has been filled with strife

I am blessed to be Jacob's wife

And to be the mother of this child

My love for him, forever wild.

HOMEWARD

With longing in his heart and weariness in his soul

Jacob set his sights upon his homeland's goal

He planned to take his family and his flocks

And return to the land of his father Isaac's stocks

Rachel, his beloved wife, was overjoyed at the thought

Of leaving her father's home where she had been brought

But in her heart, there was a fear that she couldn't shake

For she had stolen idols from her father's house to take

The idols that her father worshiped day and night

Rachel thought they were of power and of might

She thought that they could bring her blessings, and health

But she knew that Jacob's God didn't share her belief in their wealth

So she hid them in her camel's saddle, out of sight

And when her father came to search for them with might

She claimed that she could not get up from where she lay

For she was having her monthly cycle that day

And so her father left, thinking that he had failed

To find the gods that he had worshiped and hailed

But Rachel's heart was heavy with the weight of sin

For she knew that she had done something that was wrong within

She confessed to Jacob what she had done

And Jacob was angry, for he knew that he had won

All the blessings that his father had to give

And he knew that with the idols, they could not truly live

He scolded her for her mistake, but he forgave

For he knew that they were not alone in their crave

For wealth; for power; for security in life

But he reminded her that true blessings came from the God of life

And so they left her father's house with heavy hearts

Knowing that they had to make a brand new start

They traveled on the path that Jacob's God had laid

And they knew that they were blessed in every step and shade

Jacob Is Real

Once known as Jacob, I was a deceiver,

With cunning plans, I was a great achiever,

But then I wrestled with an angel one night,

And God blessed me with a brand new sight.

He saw in me a man of great worth,

And decided to give me a new birth,

Renaming me Israel, a name so grand,

To be a leader of a great new land.

I was the father of the twelve tribes,

And my descendants would grow and thrive,

A nation chosen by God above,

To show the world His mercy and love.

My name means "struggles with God",

A reminder of the path I had trod,

But now I was a man with a new mission,

To fulfill God's plan with great precision.

I learned to trust in God's ways,

To follow His lead through all my days,

And even when I stumbled and fell,

He picked me up and made me well.

My new name was a symbol of grace,

A reminder of God's loving embrace,

And though my journey was long and hard,

I knew that God was my eternal guard.

So now I look back at my life,

And I'm thankful for the struggles and strife,

For they made me the man I am today,

And led me to God's perfect way.

Greatest Wrestling Match of All Time

In the dark of night, by the Jabbok river,

Jacob was alone, his heart a quiver,

For Esau's men were drawing near,

And the thought of death was causing fear.

But suddenly, a figure appeared,

A man or angel, it wasn't quite clear,

And they wrestled on the ground,

Their struggle making an eerie sound.

Jacob fought with all his might,

Determined to win the fight,

For he knew that this was no ordinary foe,

But a messenger from God he'd come to know.

The angel grappled back with force,

But Jacob showed no signs of remorse,

He'd struggled all his life with pain,

And now he fought to earn God's name.

The night grew long, the struggle intense,

Neither one would give up the defense,

Until the angel touched Jacob's thigh,

And in that moment, he knew he'd die.

But Jacob wouldn't let go, he wouldn't relent,

He held on tight with all his strength,

And begged the angel for a blessing,

Before his fate was anything but refreshing.

The angel relented, and Jacob received,

A new name, Israel, which he believed,

Meant to struggle with God and men,

And to win the battle in the end.

Jacob had fought and won the fight,

And in the end, he saw the light,

For he knew that with God on his side,

He'd never have to run and hide.

So he limped away from the Jabbok river,

Knowing that he'd always be a giver,

Of strength and courage to all who see,

That with faith, they too can be set free.

HAPPY DAD

When Joseph was born, Israel's heart swelled,

A joy and pride he could hardly quell.

A son of his old age, a gift from above,

A symbol of God's unending love.

He held the baby with hands worn and old,

Gazing at him with a love untold.

A son to carry on his family name,

A promise of God that he would never be the same.

As Joseph grew, Israel watched with care,

Nurturing him with love and prayer.

He saw in Joseph the best of him,

A son to cherish, to protect, to win.

And as he watched Joseph mature and grow,

He knew God had a plan, a path to show.

For Joseph was destined for greatness, he could tell,

And Israel was proud, and oh so well.

He taught him the ways of their people and land,

Shared his wisdom, his faith, his command.

For Israel knew the importance of his role,

To pass on the heritage of God's ultimate goal.

And though life would have its trials and pain,

Israel knew his love for Joseph would remain.

For in his son, he saw a promise of hope,

A future for his people, a way to cope.

So he treasured each moment with his beloved boy,

Filled with gratitude, wonder, and joy.

For in Joseph, he saw a glimpse of God's grace,

And he knew his family would forever embrace.

I HAVE A DREAM

As I laid down to sleep, I had a dream so grand

The stars above were shining bright, like grains of sand

I saw myself standing tall, so proud and strong

As the stars in the sky, all bowed to me in song

I woke up with a start, my heart beating fast

Wondering what it all meant, was it just a blast?

But I couldn't shake the feeling, that this dream was true

That someday I'd be someone, that all would bow to

I shared my dream with family, but they didn't understand

They couldn't see the greatness, that lay ahead in my plan

But I knew deep in my heart, that it was meant to be

And that someday, somehow, the stars would bow to me

As time went on, my dreams were tested, and I was sold

A slave to Potiphar, my future looked so bleak and old

But I held onto my dream, and worked with all my might

And soon enough, my star was shining bright

I climbed the ranks of Egypt, and soon became a man of power

And I could see the stars aligning, with every passing hour

My family came to bow to me, just like in my dream

And I knew that everything, was exactly as it seemed

So as I lay down to sleep once again, I close my eyes and smile

For I know that dreams do come true, even if they take a while

And I thank God above, for the blessings in my life

And for the dream that gave me hope, and removed all strife.

UNFAIR

Our father's favoritism is plain to see,

Many colored coat for him, dusty rags for me.

We watch as he receives gifts and praise,

While we are left feeling envious and dazed.

Our jealousy grows with each passing day,

Our father treats Joseph better in every way.

Our anger simmers beneath the surface,

As we struggle to maintain our composure and purpose.

But then, to make matters worse,

Joseph tells us of a dream he had, oh, curse!

In his dream, he saw us bow down to him,

Our fury and resentment reached the brim.

Who does he think he is, this spoiled brat?

We will show him that he can't act like that.

We plot and scheme, our jealousy consumes us,

Our hatred for Joseph burning like a furnace.

We sell him into slavery, thinking we've won,

But in the end, we realize what we've done.

Our jealousy and envy have led us astray,

And we can't take back what we've done today.

Oh, how our jealousy blinded us,

And led us to commit this terrible injustice.

We can only hope for forgiveness and grace,

And that someday we will see Joseph's smiling face.

ENOUGH

We were twelve brothers strong,

Our love for one another did belong.

But as time passed, we grew jealous and bitter,

For Dad's favoritism towards one of us was causing a twitter.

Jealousy festered and grew within our heart,

As our father treated Joseph as a work of art.

His coat of many colors made us seethe with envy,

And we plotted against him, secretly, stealthily.

Our father doted on him with a special coat,

And praised him for every accomplishment, big or remote.

We hid the glint of envy in our eyes,

As he flaunted his dreams that he'd rise.

We plotted and schemed, we knew what to do,

To rid ourselves of this brother, oh so true.

We waited for our chance to strike,

And when it came, we didn't think twice.

We seized him and threw him into a pit,

And left him there, alone and helpless, to sit.

We discussed our options, and finally agreed,

To sell him into slavery, to satisfy our greed.

We fetched him from the pit and took him away,

Not once did we think of the price he would pay.

We met some men traveling to a destination,

So we sold Joseph to them without hesitation.

We sold him to the Ishmaelites without remorse,

Leaving Joseph alone to face his course.

He was taken far away from home,

To a land he didn't know, all alone.

We told our father a lie, to cover up our deceit,

And we watched as he wept, his heart broken and beat.

Although we've seen the last of him,

But little did we know that makes the future so grim.

Our jealousy blinded us to the bond of kin,

For in selling Joseph, we committed a great sin.

But now we feel remorse, as we see how wrong we were,

As the guilt and shame in our hearts stir.

We hope one day, our brother will forgive,

And that our family again may thrive.

For though we acted out of anger and spite,

We know our actions weren't right.

Our actions were rash, and now we see,

The weight of our guilt, and its full gravity.

We were blinded by our jealousy and pride,

And now our brother is gone, lost in the tide.

We must live with this regret, for all of our days,

And pray that God will show us mercy and grace.

May we learn from our mistakes and make amends,

And strive to be better brothers and friends.

MY GREATEST TROUBLE

My heart shattered into a million pieces,

As the news of Joseph's death reached my ears,

The pain was unbearable, the agony too deep,

And my soul couldn't hold back my tears.

My mind wandered back to the day he was born,

The joy and excitement that filled my heart,

I couldn't have imagined that my little boy

Would leave this world, and from us depart.

He was a boy with a heart full of dreams,

A ray of hope in a world full of strife.

And as I learned of his death, it seemed,

That all the colors had drained out of my life.

My sons tried to console, tried easing my pain,

But I couldn't help to feel anger, despair,

For my heart was filled with sadness, and the stain

Of grief, would never go away, no matter how much I dared.

I looked up to the heavens and cried out loud,

"Why did you take him from me, oh God above?"

And in the silence that followed, I was allowed,

To feel the weight of my loss, and to mourn my love.

In the midst of my sorrow, my days turned to night,

A small flame flickering in the dark,

What good have I earned from my tainted birthright?

I now carry Joseph's memory in my heart.

BETRAYAL REDEEMED

In my youth, my dreams were grand

Stars bowed to me, it was planned

But fate had a different hand

Betrayal awaited in the sand

My brothers looked at me with scorn

Jealousy had their hearts torn

Their hatred towards me was born

And soon, they planned to deform

I went to them, so unsuspecting

Blissfully unaware of their reckoning

The betrayal was quick and perplexing

My heart was racing, thoughts deflecting

In the pit, I felt trapped and lost

Surrounded by darkness and frost

My dreams and aspirations, a cost

Of my brothers' unforgivable exhaust

I was sold to strangers, feeling alone

My heart heavy, my future unknown

My faith in God, my only stone

As I journeyed to a land not my own

But even in the depths of despair,

God's love and guidance were always there

His hand, a light that shone everywhere

A promise of hope, beyond compare

Though I was betrayed and sold

God's plan for me would soon unfold

A destiny of greatness to behold

A story of redemption, yet to be told

Beneath the scorching sun, I walked in chains,

Sold off by brothers, full of greed and pains,

My fate unknown, my destiny unsure,

I left my home, my past, my family pure.

But in the heart of Egypt, a man of wealth,

A master to slaves, of towering health,

Bought me with gold, as if I was a prize,

To be owned and used, till the end of my demise.

My new life as a slave began,

Hard work, sweat and tears in the sand,

But even in slavery, I held onto hope

That somehow, someday, I would be able to cope.

My master, Potiphar, trusted me well,

I was in charge, and in my work did I excel,

But jealousy and lies twisted my fate,

And I was thrown into prison, left to wait.

Yet even in prison, my hope remained,

My faith unbroken, my spirit unchained,

For I knew that God had a plan for me,

To rise above my trials and be set free.

So I waited patiently, until the day,

When I was called to interpret dreams and say,

That seven years of abundance were to come,

Followed by seven years of famine and doom.

And the Pharaoh was pleased, and he raised me high,

To be his right-hand man, in power to apply,

The plan that would save Egypt, and the world beyond,

From the hunger and suffering that would take all in bond.

And so I rose from slavery to fame,

A story of hope, and a message to proclaim,

That even in the darkest hours of our life,

There's always hope, and a chance to thrive.

LUST

Oh, Joseph, son of Jacob, how fair and noble you seem,

Your presence brought joy and beauty, A light in this palace's beam.

My eyes caught your form, so gentle, And I knew I had to have you,

But you, Joseph, resisted me, refused to be untrue.

I offered you my passion, but you declined my request,

Saying, "How can I do such a thing, and sin against God who knows best?"

But I couldn't accept rejection, So I twisted the truth and lied,

Framing you with my false accusation, to satisfy my wicked pride.

You were thrown in the dungeon, an innocent man in chains,

But God was with you all along, and your faith never waned.

Oh, Joseph, son of Jacob, your trials only made you stronger,

A shining example of faith, that could last for years longer.

Through your wisdom and your patience, you rose to power in Egypt's land,

And even your betrayers, came to you with open hands.

Oh, Joseph, son of Jacob, your character was beyond compare,

And though you suffered great injustice, your faith remained steadfast and fair.

EVEN IN HERE

In the dungeon's dark and dreary cell,

A prisoner sat, lonely and unwell,

No light, no warmth, no hope in sight,

Only aching bones and endless night.

This prisoner was a man named Joseph,

Once favored, now forgotten by his people,

Betrayed by brothers, sold into slavery,

Then falsely accused, facing extreme cruelty.

In this dungeon deep and dark,

Where shadows loom and fears embark,

Joseph sat in despair and pain,

Wondering if he'd ever see the light again.

But even in the gloomiest of places,

God's grace can still reveal its traces,

And soon enough, Joseph found his way,

To success that would brighten his every day.

He became a helper to those imprisoned,

A ray of hope to those who were saddened,

His gift of interpreting dreams,

Brought comfort and relief to many extremes.

One day, two fellow inmates confided,

Their dreams that left them feeling misguided,

Joseph knew exactly what they meant,

And foretold a future that was heaven-sent.

The cupbearer was reinstated to his role,

But the baker, sadly, faced a different toll,

Joseph's predictions were fulfilled,

And his gift, in their minds, was sealed.

Though he remained in the dungeon,

Joseph's reputation began to burgeon,

And when Pharaoh had a dream to be understood,

Joseph's name was the one that was withstood.

Pharaoh, ruler of the land of Egypt,

Had two dreams that made him perplexed.

None of his wise men could give him a clue,

Or help him understand what he must do.

He dreamt of seven fat cows, grazing in the field,

And then seven gaunt cows, so weak they could barely yield.

The lean cows ate the fat cows, leaving no trace,

But they remained as thin as before in their place.

The second dream was just as strange,

Seven full ears of corn, healthy and arranged,

Then seven withered ears, thin and frail,

Devoured the good ears, leaving no trail.

Pharaoh called his wise men, but none could explain

What the dreams meant or how to avoid the pain.

Until Joseph, a prisoner, was brought before him,

Who was known for his skills of prophetic wisdom.

Joseph listened to Pharaoh and then replied,

The dreams were God's message; He would not hide.

Seven years of abundance would come to the land,

Followed by seven years of famine that would demand.

Joseph advised Pharaoh to store food and grain,

During the years of plenty, and not in vain.

So when the years of famine would arrive,

They would have enough to stay alive.

Pharaoh was overjoyed, and he quickly agreed,

To Joseph's wise plan, that would fill their need.

Joseph was appointed as a ruler of the land,

To oversee the preparation and distribution by hand.

Pharaoh knew that Joseph was a man of true insight,

Who saved the people of Egypt from their fright.

And through Joseph, God's purpose was fulfilled,

To use the famine to bring good and hope to the world.

But Satan was furious, for he had desired,

That the famine would spread, and many lives be mired.

Yet God's will could not be thwarted or stopped,

Through Joseph, His plan for redemption was topped.

Thus, even in the depths of his despair,

Joseph held onto faith, believing in prayer,

And even in the midst of darkness and pain,

He knew that hope and redemption remained.

For in the dungeon, Joseph found new strength,

As he learned to trust in a power immense,

He knew that his trials were part of a plan,

To lead him to greatness, to be a faithful man.

And so he waited, day by day,

Holding onto hope and faith to light his way,

For he knew that one day, he'd be free,

And fulfill his destiny, as God had intended it to be.

The dungeon may have been his place of sorrow,

But it also gave him hope for a brighter tomorrow,

For when he emerged, he would rise above it all,

Evermore remembered as a great leader, forever standing tall,

He rose to the position of power and might,

In a land that was once a dreadful plight.

From the darkness of the dungeon's confine,

To the shining star of Egypt, divine.

Through his perseverance and steadfast faith,

Joseph found success in the darkest place,

And through God's grace, he was able to see,

A future of prosperity, and a destiny to be.

WATCH

In the heavens high above, God spoke to his angels,

And said, "Listen to my plan, for it is full of wonders and miracles.

Pharaoh is troubled, his sleep disturbed by dreams,

And I will use them to work good out of what seems like a scheme."

The angels were all ears, curious about what God would do,

For they knew that he would never fail to make everything anew.

God said, "I will send Pharaoh two dreams, one of the cows and one of the grain,

And through them, I will show him how Joseph's sufferings is not in vain."

"He will call on Joseph to interpret his dreams,

And Joseph will use the wisdom that he gleaned,

To explain that they are a warning of seven years of famine,

And that they must prepare by storing up provisions."

The angels marveled at God's plan, for it was both just and kind,

To use Joseph's misfortunes to save all humankind.

And so they praised God, for His wisdom and His grace,

And they knew that all things worked together for good in His holy place.

                                        Satan was not pleased to hear this news

                                    This was not the reason he asked for a famine to use

                                Against these insolent humans, the growing numbers of men

                                    He wanted population control against all of them

God spoke to the angels, His chosen few,

"I'll send Pharaoh some dreams, to see it through.

The famine that's coming, is no small thing,

But with Joseph's help, it will have a good ending."

Satan was listening, with a frown on his face,

For he had a plan, to bring the human race to disgrace.

He wanted to use the famine to spread his might,

And leave the world in a terrible plight.

But God's plan was greater, it would prevail,

Satan's evil schemes, would ultimately fail.

Joseph's rise to power, in Egypt's land,

Would lead to a great saving, by God's own hand.

The famine would come, and it would be severe,

But Joseph's wisdom and guidance, would persevere.

Through the power of God, the people would survive,

And in the end, His glory would thrive.

BITTER REUNION

As Joseph stood before his brothers in disguise,

He remembered the dreams he had in his youth,

Of stars bowing down to him and fields of grain,

But now he knew those dreams had become truth.

The brothers didn't recognize him,

But Joseph knew who they were.

He could feel their presence as revenge cried from within,

Yet he opted instead to forgive.

As he listened to their conversation,

Joseph couldn't help but feel sad,

For they spoke of the brother they had sold into slavery,

And he knew they regretted hurting him and their Dad.

But Joseph chose to test them,

And sent them back home with grain,

Telling them to return with their youngest brother,

If they had to return again.

Joseph's heart was heavy as he watched them leave,

But he knew that this was all part of God's plan,

To reunite him with his family,

And teach forgiveness to all people in every land.

Amidst the grain, the silver coins did hide,

Concealed within the sack that they had bought,

The brothers trembled, fear and shame inside,

For they were certain they would soon be caught.

How had they come to this, they wondered deep,

From sons of Israel to mere thieves of grain,

With secrets kept, and bonds they could not keep,

They felt the weight of guilt and growing pain.

They went home where they all prayed,

They had enough food for all the famine days,

But slowly as time dragged on,

They realized they had all been wrong.

Israel asked them to go again

And buy more food for all of them,

They swallowed hard and then

Said they can only go back if they take Benjamin.

Israel fumed as he asked them why

When the Egyptian Governor questioned them, didn't they lie?

For still he mourned Joseph after all of these years,

To lose Benjamin too would overwhelm him with fears.

But the famine was far, far too severe,

Judah said, "Let him come with us, father dear.

I will protect him; you can rely on me.

If I fail to return him, blame me for eternity!"

But with fresh grain purchased and traveling home,

Egyptian guards surrounded like a dome,

They searched the grain sacks to find something stolen,

Each of the brothers watched their sack get opened.

A cup of silver, glinting bright,

Joseph hid it well from sight.

Into the sack of one who'd flee,

He slipped it in with secrecy.

His brothers rode on, unaware,

The cup lay hidden, nestled there.

But when they stopped to take their rest,

The cup was found, their hearts distressed.

Benjamin accused, the cup was proof,

Of stealing from the Egyptian's hoard aloof.

But one brother offered to take the blame,

For him they'd spare the rest of the frame.

The youngest brother, left behind with grief,

Had caused this journey to a foreign land,

And now their sin had brought about a thief,

And retribution by an unseen hand.

With heavy hearts, they all returned,

To Joseph, the governor they yearned.

They fell before him, and made a plea,

"Take us instead, let Benjamin free!"

But Joseph saw what they couldn't see,

The love they had for family.

He wept with joy, the truth revealed,

Their broken bonds now being healed.

He forgave them all, and let them go,

With a gift of grain to make them glow.

The cup was just a test of heart,

Their love had passed; it was a fresh start.

For in that moment, Joseph knew,

That all the pain and suffering he endured,

Was worth it, to be reunited with his family,

And to see the goodness of God's plan unfold.

HE LIVES

Israel's heart was heavy with grief,

Long had he mourned his missing chief.

Joseph, his son, so young and bright,

Taken from him, in the middle of the night.

Years had passed, and now he heard,

That Joseph was alive, not just a word,

But a real hope, a chance to see,

The son he loved, to set him free.

The news came as a shock, a surprise,

It made him question his own eyes.

Could it be true? Could Joseph live?

Or was it just a trick, a ruse to deceive?

Israel's heart was torn in two,

For he didn't know what to do.

He wanted to believe with all his might,

But could not bear to risk the sight.

Eventually, he came to know,

That it was not just a show.

Joseph was alive to tell,

In Egypt, he had fared quite well.

The thought of seeing Joseph again,

Filled him with joy, and eased his pain.

He could not wait to see his son,

And embrace him as he had done.

So he gathered up his kin,

And set out on the journey thin,

Hoping that they would find,

Peace and love with Joseph kind.

And when they finally met,

Joseph's eyes were filled and wet.

For he had waited all these years,

To see his father, and dry his tears.

Together they rejoiced and wept,

And in each other's arms embrace they kept.

For Israel had found his son,

And Joseph, a new life had begun.

AMUN RA

I am the land of Egypt,

once fertile and green,

Now dry and barren,

a wasteland it seems.

But in the midst of this famine and despair,

I hold the key to life, the gift of the harvest's share.

The world is in need, hunger and thirst,

Their crops have failed; their lands are cursed.

But here in Egypt, we have plenty to spare,

Our storehouses are full, with grain beyond compare.

People come from afar, desperate and poor,

Hoping to find refuge, to find an open door.

And we welcome them in, with warmth and with love,

Sharing our bounty, with a heart that's pure.

With each passing day, our wealth grows and grows,

Our power and influence, it overflows.

All because of the gift that we were given,

The wisdom and foresight, of the man named Joseph,

who was driven to save us, from famine and strife,

With his gift of dreams, he brought us new life.

And so we prosper, with each passing year,

Thanks to Joseph's vision, and his courage without fear.

I am the land of Egypt, and I am blessed,

With abundance and prosperity, we are truly impressed.

For in the midst of the darkest of days,

Joseph showed us his God

Who blessed us with His nod.

Amun Ra, the name we gave the God we praise.

In ancient Egypt, he reigns and stays.

He came to us in a time of need.

When famine and drought made us bleed.

Joseph, a man with divine sight,

Interpreted Pharaoh's dream right.

He stored grain and fed the land

With wisdom and skill, he took a stand.

The land of Egypt, once barren and dry,

With Joseph's help, it learned to thrive.

The Nile's waters flowed with ease;

Our stores filled, our worries ceased.

The people of Egypt were amazed

By the man who had saved their days.

They'd cried to other gods above,

But this new Amun Ra answered with love.

The new God of Egypt was born,

With his blessings, our fields were adorned.

Our hearts filled with gratitude and awe

For the miracle that we saw.

Joseph, the man who brought us wealth

Will forever be remembered with stealth.

And Amun Ra, the true God we adore,

Will be praised by our generation for evermore!

12 TRIBES BLESSED

Blessings from a father's heart

Spoken over his twelve sons

Each one with a different start

But all of them held as one.

With prophetic words he spoke

Calling out each son by name

Each of them he did invoke

To fulfill their destined claim.

Reuben, his eldest son

Honored with a double share

But his pride had come undone

His blessing came with a dare.

Simeon and Levi were fierce

Wielding violence with their hands

Their blessing came with a curse

Their anger was out of hand.

Judah, the lion's cub,

he knew would be the one to rule and reign

From him would come a line so true

His promise would not be in vain.

Zebulun, Issachar, and Dan

Each one with a task to do

And from Asher would come a clan

That would prosper and break through.

Gad, Naphtali, and Joseph too

Were blessed with land and wealth

Their destinies would all come through

And bring God's plans to perfect health.

Benjamin, the youngest son

Was blessed with strength and might

From him would come a people group

Who would always do what's right.

With his blessing spoken clear

Jacob knew his end was near

His legacy would carry through his sons

For millennia his faith still lives on.

HONORING ISRAEL

In Egypt's land, a celebration was near,

Pharaoh had made it clear,

To honor a man who was so dear,

Whose life on earth had ended here.

Jacob was the man of the hour,

A patriarch, a king with power,

Whose legacy stretched wide and far,

And reached the lands beyond afar.

By the birthright, he swindled and blessing he stole,

The famine was thwarted, saving humanity whole

The mourning had ended, and the people rejoiced,

As the memories of Jacob's life were voiced,

His journey to Egypt, his family's reunion,

His faith in God, his life's mission.

Pharaoh had granted the Hebrews their plea,

To lay Jacob to rest in Canaan, free,

And as they made it through day and night,

The Egyptians saw a wondrous sight.

A great celebration in Jacob's name,

A feast to honor his life, his fame,

Egyptians and Hebrews united as one,

To celebrate the life of Israel, the blessed son

The music played, the wine flowed,

As stories of Jacob's life were told,

The memories of him were kept alive,

As they danced and sang into the night.

Pharaoh allowed this celebration to show,

The respect he had for Jacob's glow,

And in his death, his memory lived on,

A legacy that will never be gone.

JOSEPH'S HAPPY EVER AFTER

In Egypt's land, where once he was enslaved,

Now Joseph lived, his father's legacy saved,

The ruler of Egypt, wise and just,

In his hand, the country's fate he thrust.

Years passed by, and Joseph prospered,

His wealth and power could not be measured,

His wife and children by his side,

In peace and harmony, they abide.

His brothers came to him, bowed to the ground,

And to their surprise, Joseph was found,

To be gracious and kind, forgiving and true,

Their evil deeds, he had outlived and outgrew.

His father's blessings, he had received,

And in his life, they had been achieved.

For in his heart, he held the key,

To forgiveness and love, as his father did decree.

And so Joseph lived, until his end,

A man of faith, his heart did tend,

To honor God, and serve all men,

Until the day, he joined his kin.

ZAPHNATH-PAANEAH FORGOTTEN

Joseph has so long been gone

A new Pharaoh has risen, singing a more prideful song

Amun Ra no longer revered as the only Divine One

Now demoted by men to part of a pantheon

And His history, his character, all face a downgrade

Now just a myth, a fable, phony thing that's man-made.

The Nile flows strong and wide,

A lifeline for those living beside.

But for the Hebrews, it's now a place of dread,

As Pharaoh decreed that their male babies must be dead.

Mothers weep as their infants are taken away,

To be drowned in the river before the light of day.

The cries of anguish fill the air,

As Pharaoh's soldiers carry out his cruel affair.

The river once a source of life,

Now brings death and endless strife.

The Hebrews mourn their lost sons,

While Pharaoh revels in his power won.

But even in the midst of this despair,

A ray of hope shines, however rare.

For one Hebrew mother, her love so strong,

Hides her baby boy, and he lives on.

The river may carry away so many lives,

But hope and love, it cannot deprive.

For even in the darkest hour,

God's love and hope will always flower.

www.ingramcontent.com/pod-product-compliance
Lightning Source LLC
LaVergne TN
LVHW061300060426
835509LV00016B/1656